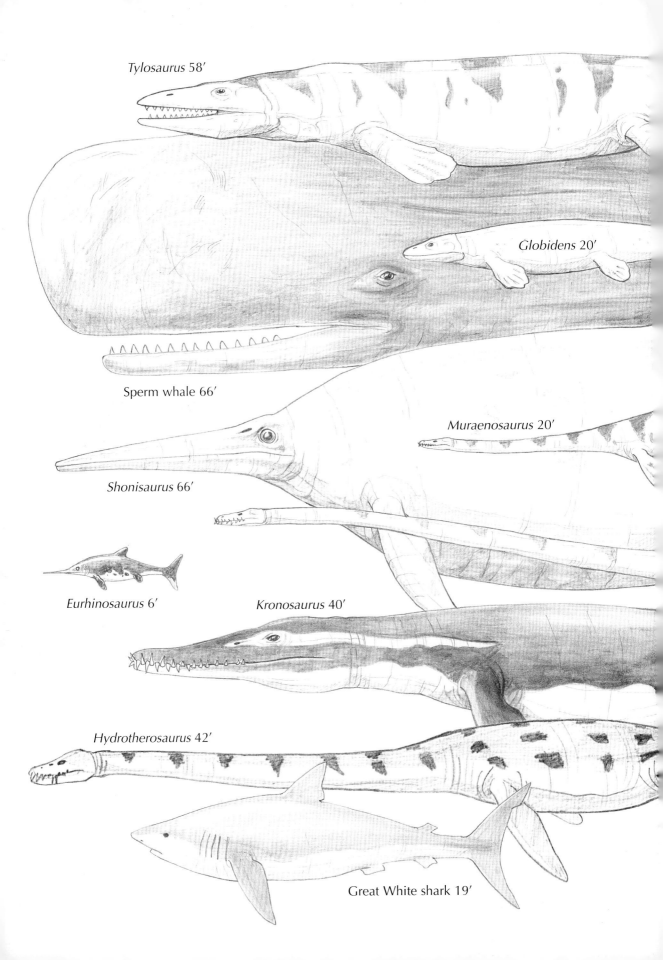

Tylosaurus 58′

Globidens 20′

Sperm whale 66′

Muraenosaurus 20′

Shonisaurus 66′

Eurhinosaurus 6′

Kronosaurus 40′

Hydrotherosaurus 42′

Great White shark 19′

Clidastes 12′

Killer whale 33′

Umoonasaurus 7′

Elasmosaurus 47′

Peloneustes 10′

Temnodontosaurus 30′

Cryptoclidus 13′

Reign *of the* SEA DRAGONS

Reign of the *SEA* *DRAGONS*

Sneed B. Collard III • *Illustrated by* **Andrew Plant**

ıкı Charlesbridge

For Bruce Weide, my friend and fellow aquatic reptile
　　　　　　　　　　　　　　　　　　—Sneed

Dedicated to Zdenek Burian, magnificent illustrator of all things prehistoric
　　　　　　　　　　　　　　　　　　—A. P.

Published by Charlesbridge
85 Main Street
Watertown, MA 02472
(617) 926-0329
www.charlesbridge.com

Library of Congress Cataloging-in-Publication Data
Collard, Sneed B.
　Reign of the sea dragons / Sneed B. Collard III ; illustrated by Andrew Plant.
　　p. cm.
　Includes index.
　ISBN 978-1-58089-124-0 (reinforced for library use)
　ISBN 978-1-58089-125-7 (softcover)
1. Marine reptiles, Fossil. 2. Paleontology—Mesozoic. I. Plant, Andrew ill. II. Title.
QE861.C785 2008
567.9'37—dc22　　　　　　　　　2007026201

Printed in China
(hc) 10 9 8 7 6 5 4 3 2 1
(sc) 10 9 8 7 6 5 4 3 2 1

Illustrations done in acrylic gouache on acid-free cartridge paper
Display type and text type set in Meridien and Optima
Color separations by Chroma Graphics, Singapore
Printed and bound by Everbest Printing Company, Ltd.,
　through Four Colour Imports Ltd., Louisville, Kentucky
Production supervision by Brian G. Walker
Designed by Diane M. Earley

Contents

The shell of an ancient marine ammonite

Into the Ancient Seas

An elasmosaur swimming through ancient seas

In a time when dinosaurs walked the earth, a strange, large animal called an *elasmosaur* (ee-LAZ-moh-sohr) slipped silently through warm ocean waters. The elasmosaur had long, elegant flippers to propel its turtle-shaped body, and a fifteen-foot neck that came in handy for sneaking up on its favorite food, squid. Soon, in fact, the elasmosaur spotted a school of squid and began swimming toward it. As it opened its jaws to strike, however, a thirty-foot-long *pliosaur* (PLEE-oh-sohr) suddenly shot up out of the depths. With its massive, seven-foot long jaws, the pliosaur seized the elasmosaur and impaled it with dozens of cone-shaped teeth. The elasmosaur struggled and thrashed to free itself, but it was no use. Soon, it died and became prey in the *food web* of the ancient ocean world.

Radical Reptiles

The elasmosaur and the pliosaur belonged to an astonishing collection of reptiles that filled our oceans during the *Mesozoic* (MEZ-oh-zoh-ik) era, about 250 to 65 million years ago. Some of these reptiles, such as crocodilians and turtles, have familiar relatives that survive today. Most, however, were totally different from anything in our modern world. They included porpoiselike *ichthyosaurs* (IK-thee-oh-sohrs), the long-necked elasmosaurs, and enormous *mosasaurs* (MOSS-uh-sohrs) with curved daggers for teeth. Scientists often refer to these reptiles as sea dragons, and they include some of the most extraordinary, awesome predators the world has ever known.

Where did they come from?

Permian Wipeout

About 245 million years ago—at the end of the *Permian* (PER-mee-un) period of the *Paleozoic* (pay-lee-uh-ZOH-ik) era—earth's oceans suffered a massive die-off, or *extinction*, of animals. Vast numbers of trilobites, fish, and other ancient marine species disappeared forever. Extinctions on land were also extensive. No one knows why these extinctions occurred. Perhaps the earth's climate changed. Maybe a colossal volcano erupted, sending deadly shockwaves across the planet and choking the skies with smoke and ash. Whatever the reason, our oceans suddenly emptied of large animals, especially predators.

The oceans didn't stay empty for long.

Over the next few million years, lizards and other reptiles began invading the seas. The oceans probably offered these reptiles abundant food supplies and, at least at first, less competition from other predators. Whatever the reason for the invasion, the reptiles' bodies and behaviors changed, or evolved, radically. Many acquired fantastic shapes and reached gigantic sizes. Eventually these reptiles dominated the marine, or ocean, environment. While the dinosaurs thundered across the continents, the sea dragons ruled the seas. After they disappeared, their stories silently slept for millions of years.

In the early nineteenth century, however, scientists began discovering the remains of these ancient marine reptiles and piecing together their lives. What have the scientists learned? It's time to find out for yourself.

WHEN THE SEA DRAGONS LIVED

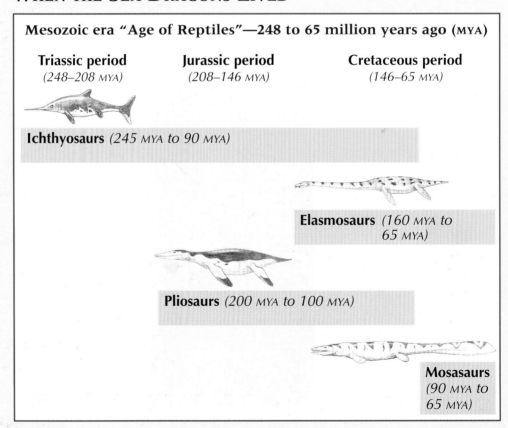

Mesozoic era "Age of Reptiles"—248 to 65 million years ago (MYA)

Triassic period (248–208 MYA)   **Jurassic period** (208–146 MYA)   **Cretaceous period** (146–65 MYA)

Ichthyosaurs (245 MYA to 90 MYA)

Elasmosaurs (160 MYA to 65 MYA)

Pliosaurs (200 MYA to 100 MYA)

Mosasaurs (90 MYA to 65 MYA)

Chapter One
Ichthyosaurs—
The Fish-Lizards

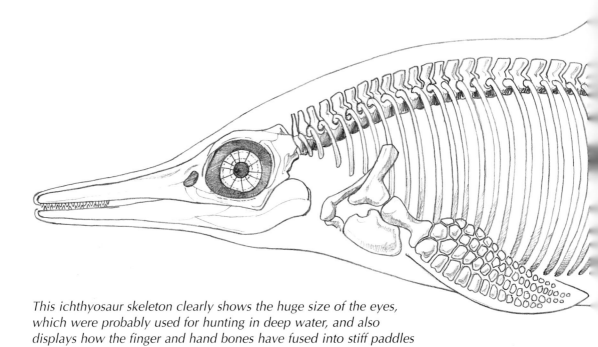

This ichthyosaur skeleton clearly shows the huge size of the eyes, which were probably used for hunting in deep water, and also displays how the finger and hand bones have fused into stiff paddles

Ichthyosaurs—Just the Facts

Name: Ichthyosaurs ("fish-lizards")

First Appearance in Fossil Record: about 245 million years ago, the Early *Triassic period* of the Mesozoic era

Last Appearance: 90 million years ago, the Middle to Late *Cretaceous* (kreh-TAY-shus) *period* of the Mesozoic era

Distribution: worldwide

Smallest size: about 2 feet long

Largest Size: about 66 feet long

Diet: mostly *cephalopods* (SEF-uh-luh-pods) and fish

Special Features: later forms were porpoise-shaped and fast; many had large eyes for hunting in deep, dark waters

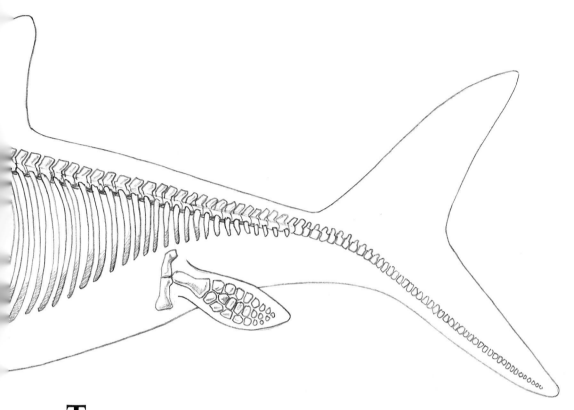

Two hundred million years ago, warm shallow seas covered huge parts of Europe, North America, and the other continents. The top predators of these ancient seas were ichthyosaurs.

Ichthyosaurs swam in all of Earth's oceans, and in some places they gathered in large numbers. Thousands of ichthyosaurs cruised the waters covering today's southern Germany. Over time many of the animals died, and their bodies sank to the sea floor where they were buried in layers of mud. Eventually this sediment hardened, trapping the dead ichthyosaurs in solid, oily slate.

For the next 200 million years, the fossilized ichthyosaurs remained sealed in their rocky tombs. But as Earth's climate cooled, large amounts of ocean waters became locked up in glaciers and polar ice caps. Sea levels dropped, and the ancient seabed became part of the land mass of Europe and was inhabited by people. About five hundred years ago, near the town of Holzmaden, Germany, people began digging up slate to use for floors and tabletops. Between the layers of this slate, they discovered the fossils of thousands of astonishing creatures.

Fish-Lizard Firsts

People mistook the first fossil ichthyosaurs for fish, and later, marine mammals. That's not surprising. Modern *paleontology* (pay-lee-un-TAWL-uh-jee)—the study of earth's past lifeforms from fossils—was still a fairly new science, and ichthyosaur skeletons did share features with both fish and mammal skeletons. In the early 1800s, however, paleontologists began carefully comparing the ichthyosaurs to the skeletons of other animals. The scientists realized that the amazing fossils weren't fish or mammals. They were reptiles. Scientists called the creatures ichthyosaurs, or "fish-lizards."

Ichthyosaurs appeared at the very beginning of the Mesozoic era, about 245 million years ago. Paleontologists aren't sure where the first ichthyosaurs came from, but early ichthyosaurs looked like

REALLY BIG ICHTHYOSAURS?

No one is sure how much ichthyosaurs weighed, but in length they usually stretched from about 2 feet long to 48-foot-long giants. Many common species were about the length of today's dolphins.

From 1998 to 2001 a paleontologist named Elizabeth Nicholls excavated a large ichthyosaur skeleton in the wilderness of British Columbia, Canada. The ichthyosaur reached a whopping 66 feet long, including a 19-foot-long skull. Nicholls named the animal *Shonisaurus sikanniensis* (sho-nih-SOHR-us sih-KAN-ee-en-sis), and its remains are housed at the Royal Tyrrell Museum in Alberta, Canada.

Shonisaurus sikanniensis

Temnodontosaurus platyodon *capturing an ancient cephalopod*

lizards. Their feet had become fins and they sported long snouts, but the bodies of these early fish-lizards were long and bendy. They probably moved through the water like a snake or an eel, and still looked very reptilian.

They wouldn't stay that way for long.

Reptilian Dolphins

Within 15 or 20 million years, ichthyosaurs lost their reptilian shapes and began to look more and more like fish. Eventually they evolved into dolphin- or tunalike animals, with short, compact bodies, smooth skin, dorsal fins for stabilization, and highly efficient crescent-shaped tails for propulsion. In a word, they were built for speed.

Like many of today's dolphins, ichthyosaurs raced through the water hunting fast-moving prey. They breathed air, like all other reptiles, but some also dove to great depths to obtain a meal. An ichthyosaur named *Temnodontosaurus platyodon* (tem-nuh-dawn-tuh-SOHR-us PLA-tee-uh-dawn) had eyes more than ten inches across—the largest eyes of any animal ever known. In deep, dark ocean waters, these huge eyes gathered enough light to detect the movement of smaller animals. With lightning snaps of their jaws, the ichthyosaurs snagged their prey and gulped them down, then returned to the surface to breathe.

The Ichthyosaur Café

Ichthyosaurs probably fed on a wide variety of prey. The fossilized scales of fish have been found in ichthyosaur stomachs. More common are the remains of cephalopods—animals with long arms covered with suckers. Living cephalopods include squid, octopuses, and nautiluses. But Mesozoic cephalopods also included *ammonites* with beautifully coiled shells, and *belemnites* (BEL-em-nites) with straight cone-shaped shells and hooks on their suckers.

Ichthyosaurs developed a special taste for these prey. An ichthyosaur's pointed, cone-shaped teeth were ideal for grasping cephalopods and, perhaps, crushing their shells. Over time some ichthyosaurs appear to have lost their teeth—evidence that these fish-lizards also sucked up and swallowed cephalopods whole.

For at least one ichthyosaur species, fish and cephalopods weren't filling enough. Unlike most other ichthyosaurs,

Eurhinosaurus, *like other ichthyosaurs and all ancient marine reptiles, breathed air just as modern marine reptiles—and mammals—do*

Temnodontosaurus eurycephalus (tem-nuh-dawn-tuh-SOHR-us yer-ee-SEF-al-us) had a short snout, massive teeth, and deep jaws that could deliver a powerful bite. What did it eat? The best guess: other ichthyosaurs.

Reptilian Respiration

Although sea life offered plenty of prey for ichthyosaurs, an ocean lifestyle came with a few problems. Breathing, for instance. Ichthyosaurs, after all, evolved from land reptiles. How could an ocean reptile get enough air, especially as it chased its prey underwater?

Scientists believe that ichthyosaurs hunting near the surface somehow took quick breaths of air. They never evolved blowholes like today's whales and dolphins have, so they had to breathe through the two airholes on their snouts or gulp air through their mouths. Ichthyosaurs may have porpoised through the water, chasing their prey and then leaping out of the water to catch a quick breath.

Deep-diving ichthyosaurs must have been able to hold their breath as many of today's dolphins and whales do. Sperm whales, for instance, can stay submerged for more than an hour as they pursue squid thousands of feet below the sea surface. Scientists believe that many ichthyosaurs did the same.

Ichthyo-Innovation

Perhaps the biggest problem ichthyosaurs faced is one shared by all marine reptiles: reproduction.

Reptiles are basically egg-laying land animals. Their eggs are covered by a shell that takes in oxygen and expels carbon dioxide and other waste gases. Reptile embryos, however, quickly drown when their eggs are submerged in water. What is a marine reptile to do?

Some early-nineteenth-century researchers suggested that female ichthyosaurs and other sea dragons hauled themselves up on beaches to lay their eggs. That is how modern sea turtles solve the

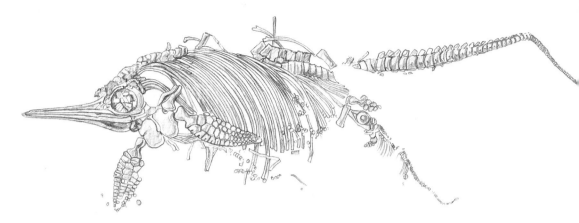

Fossil of ichthyosaur that died while giving birth

reproduction problem, so it seemed reasonable that ichthyosaurs did the same thing. Two lines of evidence, however, have pointed to a different mode of behavior.

First, several findings from the late 1800s revealed fossilized embryos in the pelvic area of adult ichthyosaurs. Second, recent studies of ichthyosaur fins have revealed that they were not strong enough to bear weight. As a result, scientists believe ichthyosaurs could never have walked or even crawled on land.

From this evidence paleontologists can only reach one reasonable conclusion. Ichthyosaurs weren't egg layers. Like modern sea snakes, ichthyosaurs evolved to give birth to live babies in the water.

This conclusion not only solves the problem of how ichthyosaurs reproduced, but it also may explain why so many ichthyosaur fossils have been found around Holzmaden and in certain other locations. Modern whales often travel to specific places to give birth. If pregnant ichthyosaurs did the same thing, it would explain the huge number of fish-lizard fossils—more than three thousand—that have been uncovered in southern Germany.

Chapter Two

Plesiosaurs Part I—
The Elasmosaurs

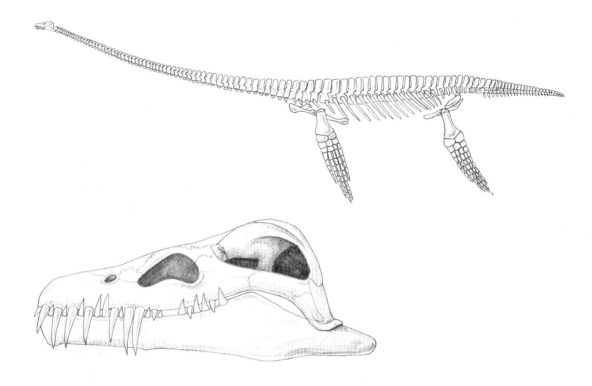

The skeleton and skull of Hydrotherosaurus *shows the large number of neck vertebrae elasmosaurs had, while the skull and teeth reveal why they were so good at snagging prey*

Elasmosaurs—Just the Facts

Name: Elasmosaurs ("thin-plated lizards," for the structure of their pelvic bones); also known as "swan lizards"

First Appearance in Fossil Record: 160 million years ago, the Late *Jurassic period* of the Mesozoic era

Last Appearance: 65 million years ago, the end of the Cretaceous period of the Mesozoic era

Distribution: worldwide, perhaps more in cooler waters

Smallest Size: 4 or 5 feet long

Largest Size: about 47 feet long

Diet: primarily cephalopods and fish

Special Features: known for their extremely long necks and slow swimming; also known for having eyes close together, giving them binocular vision for better depth perception

One day in December 1823, twenty-four-year-old Mary Anning was searching for fossils along the cliffs of her home in Lyme Regis, England. The cliffs were made of white chalk that had been deposited on the ancient sea floor, and were well-known for containing ammonites and other fossil animals. But on this day Anning's keen eyes spotted something no one had ever seen before. It was a complete skeleton of a large animal with a short turtle-shaped body, four long flippers, and a medium-length tail. Most extraordinary was its neck. It stretched almost half of the animal's entire length and supported a small, compact head.

Anning prepared the fossil and handed it over to famed English paleontologist William Daniel Conybeare, who named the new animal *Plesiosaurus dolichodeirus* (PLEE-zee-uh-sohr-us doe-lik-oh-DEER-us) or "near-lizard, long-necked." Not everyone believed the new discovery. When one famous French scientist heard about it, he thought the *plesiosaur* (PLEE-zee-uh-sohr) was a made-up animal. But it was no hoax. It was the first of dozens of plesiosaur species that would be discovered during the next two centuries.

The Long-Necks

Like other sea dragons, plesiosaurs evolved from land reptiles. They swam the seas from about 230 million to 65 million years ago, and came in a huge variety of shapes and sizes. Scientists divide plesiosaurs into several groups, but two groups stand out. One contains the savage predators known as pliosaurs, which had shorter necks and massive skulls. (You'll meet them in the next chapter.) Just as captivating were the elasmosaurs, plesiosaurs that had long—very long—necks. The elasmosaurs appeared about 160 million years ago.

Humans have only seven neck bones, but some large elasmosaurs had more than seventy. Just how elasmosaurs used their long necks has been debated for nearly two centuries. People used to think that elasmosaurs swam at the ocean's surface in order to breathe, their necks held up in the air like a swan's. In early depictions, they were

THE LEGACY OF MARY ANNING

Mary Anning has been called "the greatest fossilist the world ever knew." During her lifetime she collected thousands of important fossils that were eagerly sought by the greatest scientists of her day. Anning had almost no formal education, but became a world expert on ancient species through reading and keen observation. "The extraordinary thing in this young woman," a woman who knew her wrote, "is that she has made herself so thoroughly acquainted

Mary Anning

with the science that the moment she finds any bones she knows to what tribe they belong." Besides her discovery of the first plesiosaur fossils, Anning and her brother discovered England's first ichthyosaur skeleton in around 1810. If that wasn't enough, in 1828 Mary discovered the first known remains of the flying reptile pterodactyl (tehr-a-DAK-til). Together her finds have fascinated scientists and left a lasting legacy of knowledge about life on Earth.

often shown this way, looking down into the water for food. Other scientists thought the animals' necks could wrap and twist around like a snake so that elasmosaurs could coil and strike at their prey.

Probably neither of these images is true. Some elasmosaurs grew to only four or five feet long, but others were forty-five-foot-long giants with necks weighing several hundred pounds. To hold such a neck up in the air would have made the elasmosaur's body impossibly unstable in the water—and would have required Herculean strength.

Scientists are not in complete agreement on the neck's flexibility. In a recent text one scientist wrote that an elasmosaur's neck "could bend around upon itself two or three times." With such a neck, the animal could have seized fish without moving the body at all. However, other scientists have observed that an elasmosaur's neck *vertebrae* fit too tightly together to allow the neck to bend very much. They also point out that the muscles at the base of the neck were too thick to be very flexible.

But if that long neck didn't bend or stick up in the air, what use was it?

Full Speed (Straight) Ahead

Most paleontologists now believe that elasmosaurs swam with their necks stretched out in front of them, or perhaps above and in front of them. According to this view, the advantage of the neck was not that it could twist and coil or let the animal look down from above. Instead it allowed elasmosaurs to hide their enormous main bodies, or trunks, while they were hunting. The sight of a huge body with four long flippers would have frightened away most prey. But with a long neck, an elasmosaur could sneak up on schools of prey while keeping its main trunk hidden behind or below it.

Scientists generally agree that elasmosaurs fed mostly on fish and cephalopods. Recently, however, two Australian scientists discovered the remains of clams, snails, and crabs in the stomach regions of two

The comparatively small heads and long necks of elasmosaurs like Muraenosaurus *probably helped them get close to their prey*

elasmosaur fossils. This indicates that elasmosaurs may also have used their long necks to pluck food off the ocean bottom.

Elasmosaurs used their long, flexible flippers as wings and flew through the water as penguins and sea turtles do today.

Elasmosaurs probably weren't fast swimmers, but with their sneaky ways and bottom-dwelling prey, they didn't have to be.

Thanks to their long necks, they could approach their prey without being detected. Using quick strikes and meshed rows of sharply pointed teeth, the elasmosaurs impaled or trapped their victims before gulping them down whole.

The elasmosaur Cryptoclidus *collecting gastroliths to aid in digestion*

Rockin' Out

Early fossil hunters quickly noticed something unusual about elasmosaur skeletons: they often had piles of stones, now called *gastroliths* (GAS-truh-liths), sitting in the stomach area. The stones ranged in size from pebbles to rocks the size of baseballs, and they were often polished smooth. One elasmosaur contained twenty-nine pounds of stones. It had obviously swallowed them on purpose, but why?

Some scientists have speculated that the stones served as ballast. Ships often carry extra weight in their hulls to give them stability as they sail through rough seas. Perhaps the gastroliths helped keep an elasmosaur's body stable as it swam, or acted as a weight belt so it could dive down after prey. The problem with this theory is the elasmosaur's size. The biggest elasmosaurs grew up to forty-five feet long and weighed as much as fourteen thousand five hundred pounds. For an animal this heavy, twenty-nine pounds of additional weight probably wouldn't be much help.

A more likely explanation for gastroliths is that they helped grind an elasmosaur's prey. Paleontologists have found tiny, broken-up fish bones and scales among some piles of gastroliths—evidence that the stones did, in fact, help break up elasmosaur food. This isn't too surprising, since modern crocodilians also rely on gastroliths to aid in digestion.

One challenge for elasmosaurs was finding the right stones. Gastroliths recovered by scientists show that elasmosaurs preferred certain kinds of rocks—especially those made of quartz—over others. The seas where elasmosaurs spent most of their time, however, had muddy bottoms. By comparing fossil locations to the nearest sources of gastroliths, scientists have concluded that some elasmosaurs swam to special "quarries" hundreds of miles away. They may even have swum up rivers to find just the right kinds of stones for their digestive needs.

Elasmo-Babies

The mystery of how ancient marine reptiles reproduced has been debated by many scientists. The discovery of fossilized embryos solved the riddle for ichthyosaurs, but what about other groups of sea dragons? Even in the last few years some amateur plesiosaur lovers have suggested that plesiosaurs dragged themselves up onto

The elasmosaur Hydrotherosaurus *giving birth to a live baby*

the beach to lay eggs. But modern scientists who study plesiosaur skeletons believe this would have been impossible for an animal built like a plesiosaur—or any of the other sea dragons.

As paleontologist Michael Everhart puts it, "It appears likely that live birth is one of the necessary *adaptations* that egg-laying reptiles had to make in order to successfully return to life in the ocean." Discovery of fossilized embryos in one plesiosaur species backs up Everhart's ideas. And if ancient marine reptiles gave birth to live babies, they probably provided parental care to their young to help ensure their survival. Whole pods of plesiosaurs may have swum together, the mothers—and perhaps fathers—guiding their babies to food sources and protecting them against giant sharks and other predators.

If Earth's history had been only a little different, we might be paying to go on plesiosaur-watching trips instead of the whale-watching cruises we take today.

COPE'S "BACKWARD" ELASMOSAUR

The discovery of ancient marine reptiles inspired great competition among paleontologists. The most famous rivalry was between Edward Drinker Cope and Othniel Charles Marsh. In the mid-nineteenth century, the two scientists raced all over the American West, trying to outdo each other with their discoveries, and even paid others to obtain fossils first. Their rivalry led to huge embarrassment for one of them. When a doctor named Theophilus Turner discovered a plesiosaur skeleton in Kansas, Cope asked him to ship the fossil to Philadelphia for examination. Right away Cope realized it was a long-necked plesiosaur and rushed to reassemble the skeleton and publish his results. In his haste Cope made a critical mistake: he placed the head of the elasmosaur on the end of its tail! To make matters worse, his arch-rival Marsh helped discover the mistake. Cope quickly corrected his error, but the word was out. He would have to live with the ridicule of his "backward plesiosaur" for the rest of his life.

Edward Drinker Cope

Chapter Three

Plesiosaurs Part II—
The Pliosaurs

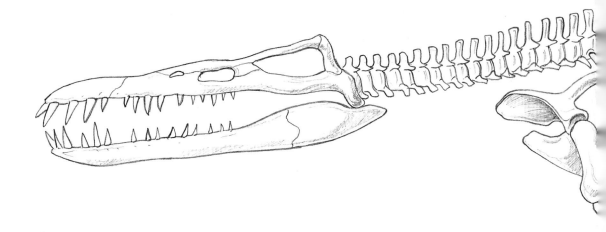

This Liopleurodon *pliosaur skeleton shows a more compact body—and much larger mouth—than its elasmosaur cousins*

Pliosaurs—Just the Facts

Name: Pliosaurs ("more lizardlike")

First Appearance in Fossil Record: About 200 million years ago, the Early Jurassic period of the Mesozoic era

Last Appearance: About 100 million years ago, the early Late Cretaceous period of the Mesozoic era

Distribution: worldwide

Smallest Size: porpoise-sized, 4 to 6 feet long

Largest Size: at least 35 feet long, perhaps 50 feet or more

Diet: large cephalopods, fish, plesiosaurs, and other marine reptiles

Special Features: ferocious predators known for short necks, massive jaws, and fast swimming

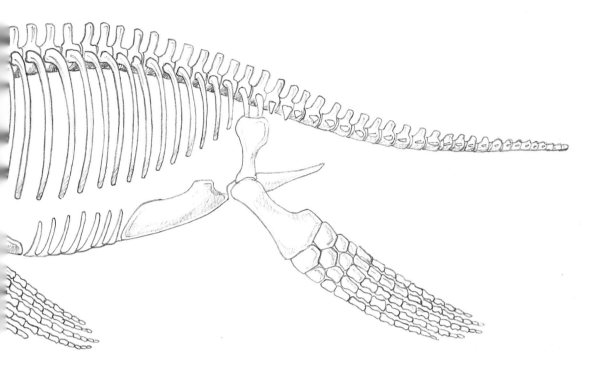

Elasmosaurs were not the only impressive plesiosaurs cruising ancient seas. Even more awesome were their close cousins, the pliosaurs. In his book *Sea Dragons: Predators of Prehistoric Oceans*, biologist Richard Ellis writes, "The pliosaurs were probably the most terrifying marine predators that ever lived. They dominated the seas the way the carnivorous dinosaurs dominated the land."

Pliosaurs were perfectly adapted to attack, kill, and eat large, meaty prey. Like elasmosaurs, they had thick main bodies, long fins, and fairly short tails. But pliosaurs evolved shorter necks that supported long, heavy heads with big mouths. Some may have fed on smaller cephalopods and fish, but the pliosaurs' main menu featured large sharks, squid, elasmosaurs, ichthyosaurs, and other pliosaurs. To understand what made pliosaurs such efficient killing and eating machines, we need look no further than a giant pliosaur from Down Under.

Kronosaurus

In 1931 and 1932 a group of zoologists from Harvard University traveled to Queensland, Australia, to look for fossils. They weren't disappointed. On their trip, they found the remains of an enormous pliosaur at least thirty-five feet long. Its name: *Kronosaurus queenslandicus* (kroh-nuh-SAUR-us kweenz-LAN-dih-kus).

Kronosaurus queenslandicus had actually been discovered in 1899, but the first specimen consisted only of a lower jaw, some teeth, and a few other bones. The Harvard discovery was almost complete, and it showed what a fearsome predator *Kronosaurus* was.

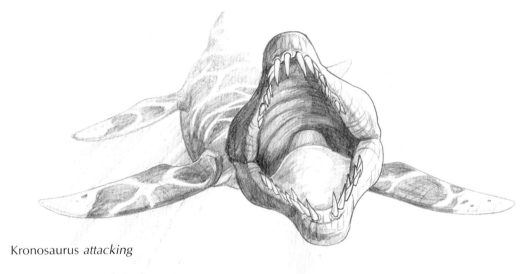

Kronosaurus *attacking*

While elasmosaurs were content to cruise slowly through the water, *Kronosaurus* and other pliosaurs raced after their prey. Both elasmosaurs and pliosaurs had long fins, but pliosaur fins were more rigid, allowing them to generate greater speed with each stroke. Pliosaurs evolved massive shoulder bones that allowed the attachment of large muscles to drive the fins forward. An impressive heart and large lungs powered vigorous swimming activity.

The name *Kronosaurus* comes from the Greek mythological figure Kronos, who ate his children. It is doubtful that this animal did the same, but it didn't hesitate to devour all manner of other prey. *Kronosaurus*'s heavy jaws held rows of eleven-inch teeth— longer than the canines of saber-toothed cats. With these teeth *Kronosaurus* subdued ammonites, turtles, large fish, and even other

ERIC, THE SEMI-PRECIOUS PLIOSAUR

In 1986 in South Australia, a miner named Joe Vida unearthed one of the most unusual fossils ever found—an almost complete pliosaur skeleton that had been *opalized.* Opals are valuable gems that are created by a geological process that replaces minerals with silica. No one, however, had ever found an opalized sea dragon. The pliosaur was about six feet long and even contained the opalized remains of fish and gastroliths. After it was reconstructed, it was put up for auction for $300,000. The curator of paleontology at the Australian Museum decided to try to buy the opal pliosaur for the museum through a public fund-raising effort. It worked. Individuals and corporations raised more than $340,000 so that the pliosaur— named "Eric"— would always be on display for all Australians to enjoy.

The pliosaur Umoonasaurus—*the same species as the opalized "Eric"*

large marine reptiles. Scientists believe that *Kronosaurus* probably rushed up at its prey from below, as great white sharks do today. For the largest prey, *Kronosaurus* may have used "bolt-shake feeding," seizing its victim and violently shaking it back and forth, ripping it apart with its terrifying teeth.

How big an animal could *Kronosaurus* kill? In 1982 scientists discovered the remains of a thirty-foot-long fossil elasmosaur called *Woolungasaurus glendowerensis* (wool-UN-guh-sohr-us glen-dow-er-REN-sis). The animal's skull had been crushed, and even more amazing, it showed bite marks from an enormous predator. Scientists concluded that *Woolungasaurus* had been killed by none other than *Kronosaurus.*

Super Senses

Like modern predators, *Kronosaurus* and other sea dragons must have relied on keen senses to capture their prey. Most sea dragon fossils have left behind bony *sclerotic* (skluh-RAH-tic) *rings* of hardened tissue. Sclerotic rings were used to focus the eyes, and they give a good idea of how big an animal's eyeballs were. From these sclerotic rings and the large eyes on many sea dragons, scientists can safely conclude that vision was essential to almost all species of sea dragons.

Unfortunately, sensory organs are usually made of soft tissues that are almost never preserved in fossils. Paleontologists must make educated guesses about most senses based on indirect evidence. The nostrils of the pliosaur called *Pliosaurus,* for instance, were too small to breathe through, so scientists believe that *Pliosaurus* and other pliosaurs used their nostrils to smell or taste underwater. Other kinds of sea dragons also could probably taste or smell—an extremely useful feature for detecting prey and enemies.

Several scientists have wondered if pliosaurs and other ancient marine reptiles hunted using *echolocation*—an adaptation found in bats and marine mammals. When echolocating, an animal makes a noise and listens for the delay and direction of the echo. This allows the animal to detect the location of prey and other objects. For echolocation to work, however, an animal's ears have to be separate from its braincase, so that each ear can get a clear, distinct signal from an incoming sound. A scientist named Michael Taylor studied the problem in one species of pliosaur and wrote, "The ears were not acoustically isolated from the braincase, so underwater directional hearing was poor." Other scientists have reached the same conclusion for ichthyosaurs. As wonderfully adapted as the sea dragons were to ocean life, it seems that echolocation probably was not part of their sensory toolkits.

Running Hot and Cold

An even bigger debate about both dinosaurs and ancient marine reptiles such as pliosaurs is whether or not they were *endothermic,* or warm-blooded. Both mammals and birds are endothermic. We humans, for instance, manufacture our own body heat, and that ability allows our inside body chemistry to always function at the same controlled temperature.

Peloneustes—*a transitional form between longer and shorter necked pliosaurs*

The vast majority of today's reptiles, on the other hand, are cold-blooded, or *ectothermic*. They must rely on the sun or on air or water temperatures to provide them with the heat they need to operate. What about pliosaurs and other sea dragons? Were they warm- or cold-blooded? The answer may not be black-and-white.

Some scientists believe that sea dragons operated just fine as ectotherms, and that their body chemistries had adapted to function well at different temperatures. Other scientists disagree. Paleontologist Chris McGowan believes that the fast swimming speeds of ichthyosaurs indicates that they were warm-blooded like today's tunas. While most fish are cold-blooded, tunas have evolved a heat-exchange system that keeps heat in their bodies and raises their body temperatures. Perhaps ichthyosaurs, pliosaurs, and other sea dragons operated under a similar system.

The huge size of many sea dragons also suggests that they retained body heat quite well. Their bodies may not have generated heat chemically like ours do, but simple muscle activity may have produced heat as a by-product. This heat may have kept the animals' bodies warmer, and almost by accident, led to a different sort of warm-bloodedness. Such a system is found in modern leatherback sea turtles. Leatherback turtles can reach lengths of ten feet and weights of two thousand pounds. Their sheer mass allows them to maintain raised body temperatures, even in arctic and other cold waters.

Scientists may never know for sure if ancient marine reptiles were endotherms or ectotherms, but either way, the sea dragons seemed to have no trouble coping with whatever conditions the Mesozoic dished out.

WHAT COLORS WERE ANCIENT MARINE REPTILES?

Skin is almost never preserved in fossils, and even when it is, it contains no true indication of color. Scientists believe, however, that like almost all of today's living animals, sea dragons did come in an assortment of patterns and colors. Today's fish, turtles, and marine mammals often exhibit *countershading*.

Their top, or dorsal, surfaces are dark, while their bottom, or ventral, surfaces are pale. This camouflages these animals from above and below. When viewed from above, the top surface of a countershaded animal blends in with the darker waters around it. When seen from below, the pale ventral surface blends in with the bright light coming down from the water's surface.

Still, there's simply no way to know what colors sea dragons came in. It's a good guess that sea dragons showed at least some of the same color ranges that today's marine reptiles display. If we could step back into a time machine, it wouldn't be too surprising to find sea dragons dressed in a wide assortment of green, blue, brown, and gray skins. Various ancient marine reptiles probably also exhibited bars, stripes, spots, and other features to help them blend in with their environments.

Possible pliosaur patterns

Chapter Four
The Mosasaurs

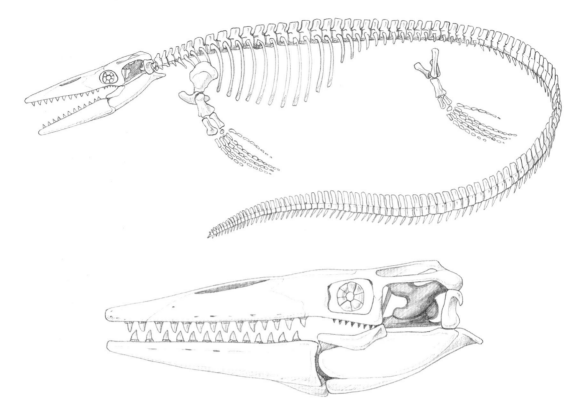

Looking at the skeleton and skull of the mosasaur Tylosaurus, *showing jaw hinge and palatal teeth, it's not hard to see that mosasaurs evolved from lizards*

Mosasaurs—Just the Facts

Name: Mosasaurs ("Meuse River lizard," after the location in the Netherlands where the first mosasaur was discovered in 1780)

First Appearance in Fossil Record: About 90 million years ago, the Middle Cretaceous period of the Mesozoic era

Last Appearance: About 65 million years ago, the end of the Cretaceous period and the Mesozoic era

Distribution: worldwide

Smallest Size: less than 12 feet long

Largest Size: 58 feet long

Diet: cephalopods, fish, turtles, shellfish, birds, plesiosaurs, other mosasaurs

Special Features: more lizardlike than other sea dragons; evolved into a huge variety of species

In 1804, while exploring a cliff above the Missouri River, members of the Lewis and Clark expedition encountered "the back-bone [*sic*] of a fish forty-five feet long, tapering towards [*sic*] the tail, and in a perfect state of petrifaction." They made the find in what is now the state of South Dakota, and as their journals indicate, they weren't sure what they were looking at. They thought it was the remains of a fish, or perhaps a snake. They did send part of a fossil back to Washington, D.C., for identification. Unfortunately, the sample was lost, so scientists of that time could not be sure from their description what the fossil was. Today paleontologists believe that their discovery was even more exciting than a new kind of fish or snake. Lewis and Clark had most likely stumbled across America's first known fossil of a mosasaur.

Make Way for Mosasaurs

The sea dragons known as mosasaurs didn't show up until late in the Mesozoic era, but they arrived with a splash. Up until 90 million years ago, no mosasaurs swam in Mesozoic seas. Then suddenly, they were everywhere.

Why they showed up so suddenly is a bit of a mystery, but scientists believe that it had to do with the decline of other ancient marine reptiles. Ichthyosaurs had all but disappeared by about 90 million years ago. Plesiosaurs had also been losing ground to

Clidastes—an early mosasaur

advanced species of sharks and other fish. The time was right for a new invasion of the seas, and mosasaurs seized the opportunity.

Scientists have not identified the ancestors of other sea dragons, but they have a pretty good idea where mosasaurs came from. Paleontologists believe that mosasaurs evolved from small land lizards such as aigialosaurs (eg-ee-AHL-uh-sohrz) that lived close to the ocean. About 95 million years ago, these lizards began moving into the sea, and within 4 or 5 million years, they acquired a host of adaptations for an ocean existence.

New Twists

Mosasaurs share many features with other ancient marine reptiles. They hunted many of the same prey. Their legs evolved into flippers. They were probably helpless on land, and they almost

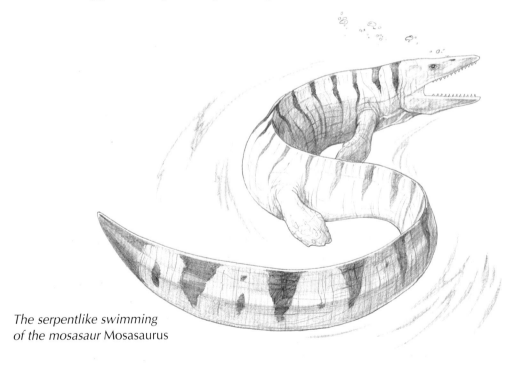

The serpentlike swimming of the mosasaur Mosasaurus

certainly gave birth to live babies in the water—probably four or five at a time. They also appear to have colonized most, if not all, of the world's oceans.

Mosasaurs, however, added their own features to ocean life. For one thing, they kept their reptilian good looks. Ichthyosaurs evolved to look like dolphins. Plesiosaurs looked like, well, nothing else. But mosasaurs looked very much like modern lizards or crocodilians. Their long flattened tails stretched at least half their body lengths, and like ichthyosaurs, mosasaurs used these tails to propel themselves through the water. While ichthyosaurs evolved stiff tunalike bodies, however, mosasaur bodies remained more flexible, giving the animals a more snakelike appearance as they swam through the water.

Mosasaurs also kept their scales, at least early on. Ichthyosaurs and plesiosaurs seemed to have evolved smooth skins like a dolphin's, but fossils of early mosasaurs clearly show that they were covered with thousands of tiny diamond-shaped scales like those of modern snakes and *monitor lizards*.

Lightning Strike

Paleontologists are amazed by how quickly and completely mosasaurs took over ancient seas. Paleontologist Michael Everhart writes, "Other groups of reptiles had also enjoyed limited successes in the oceans of the Mesozoic, but none approached the worldwide domination of the seas that mosasaurs would attain in the Late Cretaceous."

Part of the mosasaurs' success lies in their enormous size. One early group, called *tylosaurs* (TIE-luh-sohrz), grew to lengths of almost forty-five feet. They had heavy, cone-shaped teeth that helped them subdue plesiosaurs and other mosasaurs. Scientists have also gathered evidence that tylosaurs dived to great depths to hunt giant squid.

Many other species of mosasaurs also reached immense lengths. Most mosasaurs seemed to prefer living in food-rich coastal waters, but their huge sizes also allowed them to safely cruise the open ocean, where many of them apparently gave birth. Near the end of the Mesozoic, at least two species of mosasaurs even invaded estuaries and freshwater rivers—a stronghold of ancient crocodilians.

How did they do it?

The Mosasaur Menu

Mosasaurs couldn't swim fast for long periods of time like ichthyosaurs did, but they could probably sprint for short distances. Like plesiosaurs, they were "ambush predators," surprising their prey and then chasing them down in a quick sprint. What did they eat? A better question is, what *didn't* they eat?

"Mosasaurs probably fed primarily on fish and cephalopods such as squid and belemnites," writes Michael Everhart, "but the fossil record shows that they would have eaten just about anything they could swallow." In the stomach of a single *Tylosaurus* (TIE-luh-sohr-us), scientists discovered the remains of a shark, a bony fish, a swimming bird, and a smaller mosasaur. Other menu items included ammonites, plesiosaurs, and turtles.

To catch, kill, and swallow these prey, many mosasaurs had stout, pointed teeth that were curved slightly toward the rear of the mouth. These teeth couldn't tear up food, but they did help guide prey down a mosasaur's throat. To assist in the swallowing process, mosasaurs had two additional rows of teeth on their *palates*. These extra teeth kept prey from slipping away as the mosasaurs gulped it down.

The ball-shaped teeth of Globidens *crushed shelled animals with ease*

As time went on, some mosasaurs became more specialized. Several smaller mosasaurs evolved hard rounded teeth ideal for crushing clams, sea urchins, and other shellfish. Scientists believe that one fifty-foot-long giant named *Hainosaurus* (HAYN-uh-sohr-us) evolved into a particularly deadly killing machine. It had a large solid nose that it may have used to smash into skulls of other mosasaurs, killing them. Unlike other mosasaurs, *Hainosaurus* had teeth that were *serrated* for cutting or slicing apart its prey. Its mouth could also expand to swallow unusually large chunks of meat, as well as whole turtles and other large prey.

MESOZOIC IDOLS OF THE VICTORIAN AGE

Today dinosaurs get much more attention than ancient marine reptiles, but that hasn't always been the case. The first sea dragon fossils were identified several years before the first dinosaurs, and the word "dinosaur" was not even coined until 1842. Meanwhile, sea dragons earned an avid early following in Europe and North America, where collectors paid high prices for ichthyosaur and plesiosaur fossils. When the French invaded the Netherlands in 1795, the French army seized the first known mosasaur fossil from its Dutch owner and shipped it to a well-known scientist in Paris. In the 1850s, at the famous Crystal Palace Park in south London, workers reconstructed life-size models of huge marine reptiles alongside dinosaurs. Over time dinosaurs surpassed sea dragons in popularity. But if this book shows anything, it's that sea dragons once again deserve to share the spotlight.

The life-size—although somewhat inaccurate—Crystal Palace Park models of a plesiosaur and an ichthyosaur

The Last Hurrah

By about 85 million years ago, mosasaurs outnumbered plesiosaurs by more than ten to one. Life was not perfect, of course. Large fish and other marine reptiles preyed on young mosasaurs. Enormous sharks up to thirty feet long probably even attacked adult mosasaurs. One of the most fearsome fishes was the ginsu shark, *Cretoxyrhina manteli* (kreh-tox-ee-RINE-uh man-TEH-lye). Reaching the size of today's largest great white sharks, the ginsu shark came armed with hundreds of razor teeth two inches long. Paleontologists have found these teeth embedded in the bones of many mosasaur fossils.

Young mosasaurs often fell prey to ancient sharks such as Cretoxyrhina

Even with large sharks swimming around, however, Mesozoic life was probably pretty good for the mosasaurs. During the time that *Tyrannosaurus rex* (tye-RAN-oh-sohr-us rex) terrorized the land, mosasaurs ruled the ancient seas. They had plenty to eat. Their enemies were few. To paraphrase the title of a popular song, their future was so bright they had to wear shades.

But then, in a geological instant, it all came to an end.

Chapter Five
Extinction

People have been mystified by the disappearance, or extinction, of dinosaurs ever since their fossils were first discovered in the early 1800s. The extinction of the sea dragons is just as perplexing. Scientists date the disappearance of both groups to the *K-T extinction event* that occurred 65 million years ago. During this event, 85 percent of all species on earth disappeared. But while the K-T extinction probably wiped out mosasaurs and the last of the plesiosaurs, it does not explain why all sea dragons disappeared.

Ichthyo-Troubles

Ichthyosaurs were the first sea dragons to evolve—and the first to disappear. The last ichthyosaurs became extinct almost 30 million years *before* the K-T event. Climate may have played some role in ichthyosaur extinctions. Scientists who study the fossil record have observed that when global temperatures rose, more ichthyosaur species flourished. When temperatures fell, their numbers declined. However, an even bigger issue for ichthyosaurs—as for most animal and plant species—was competition.

While ichthyosaurs were swimming the seas, new groups of faster, more efficient fish were also evolving. The larger of these fish—including the sharks—probably began preying on ichthyosaur young. Perhaps more important, many of the bony fish had now evolved efficient, streamlined bodies that could match the speed of the ichthyosaurs. These faster fish became harder for icthyosaurs to hunt, and also started outswimming ichthyosaurs for all kinds of prey.

These factors spelled doom for the ichthyosaurs. By the middle of the Cretaceous, about 93 million years ago, only one major group of ichthyosaurs remained. Then, unable to adapt to the changing world, this group vanished, too.

Plesiosaur Dolichorhynchops *killed by a mosasaur*

Plesiosaur Problems

Unlike ichthyosaurs, plesiosaurs ambushed their prey. This allowed both elasmosaurs and pliosaurs to survive in an ocean full of faster fish. But soon plesiosaurs would face their own problem, and its name was mosasaur. About the time that mosasaurs invaded the seas, the number of plesiosaurs plummeted. They completely vanished from waters far out at sea while closer to shore only a few species survived.

Like ichthyosaurs, plesiosaurs may have suffered competition from faster, more efficient fish. But it's also likely that the newer mosasaurs simply were better at ocean life than the plesiosaurs. Mosasaurs definitely preyed on plesiosaurs, and they may also have been better at catching food. A few plesiosaurs figured out ways to survive, but as Michael Everhart writes, "Plesiosaurs were probably losers of an evolutionary arms race." In the years before the K-T event, they'd already boarded the train for Extinctionville.

Mosasaurs and Meteors

Scientists have no reason to believe that mosasaurs were also heading toward extinction at the close of the Mesozoic era. In fact the opposite seems true. Mosasaurs had successfully conquered ancient seas, and even better, they were adaptable. Mosasaur biology seemed perfectly suited to dealing with any changes that came along.

Any changes except one.

No one knows exactly what caused the massive K-T extinction event that wiped out dinosaurs, sea dragons, and most other life on earth. In theory K-T could have been caused by rapid climate change, volcanic activity, disease—or a combination of factors. Many scientists, however, point their fingers toward space.

A huge asteroid may have ended the reign of both sea dragons and dinosaurs—and changed life on our planet

Paleontologists have good evidence that a huge asteroid slammed into Earth about 65 million years ago in the region of Mexico's Yucatan Peninsula. This asteroid was about six miles across and must have devastated Earth's environment. The actual impact and explosion of the asteroid would have killed off thousands— perhaps millions—of species. It's also likely that the impact sent up a thick cloud of debris and dust that choked earth's atmosphere for years, blocking out most sunlight and creating intense acid rain. In such a darkened, polluted world, most plant life would have perished. This, in turn, would have devastated entire food webs.

Reduced sunlight might also have triggered much colder temperatures, wiping out the millions of species that were adapted to the warm climate of the Mesozoic. The eruption of massive volcanoes would have produced similar devastating results. Whatever caused it, K-T changed life on this planet forever. It exterminated dinosaurs, sea dragons, and millions of other species. If K-T hadn't happened, we might live in a world still inhabited by megareptiles.

Then again, some people believe that these animals didn't entirely disappear. . . .

After the Impact

A growing number of researchers believe that at least a few dinosaurs and sea dragons survived the K-T event. If so, where are they?

Most scientists believe that birds began evolving from dinosaurs well before K-T. Birds show many features common to dinosaurs, and several fossils also have been found that look like transition species between dinosaurs and modern birds. This suggests that, in their way, some dinosaurs not only survived K-T, they adapted to thrive in our modern world.

Similarly, some paleontologists think that before K-T, some mosasaurs began evolving into today's snakes and monitor lizards. If you look at a snake or a Komodo dragon, they look very much like the fossils of mosasaurs. Their scales have similar shapes. Both snakes and mosasaurs share hinged jaws that allow them to swallow large prey. Snakes also have teeth on their palates, just like mosasaurs.

Other scientists reject the idea that snakes descended from mosasaurs, saying that snakes traveled their own evolutionary path, and that mosasaurs did indeed disappear forever. As scientists continue to study ancient species, our knowledge of these animals and their relationships will continue to grow. Paleontologists are constantly searching for new fossils that are missing links between major animal groups. It is quite possible that someone—maybe even

The fossilized remains of sea dragons teach us about their world

you—will discover a fossil animal that reveals vital information about mosasaurs and the animals that evolved from them.

Each new piece of information will only add to our awe of ancient sea dragons. For 180 million years these spectacular creatures dominated our oceans in ways that seem almost impossible. If we didn't see their fossil remains for ourselves, we'd never believe that such animals existed. But they did. And even 65 million years later, they not only fire our imaginations, they drive us to learn more about the incredible power of evolution and the miracle of life on earth.

Learning More About Sea Dragons

Books

When I first considered writing this book, I knew it would be a challenge, because very little had recently been published about sea dragons. I began diving into scientific papers, trying to get an overall picture of these animals and what made them so interesting. Then all of a sudden, two great books were published.

The first was *Sea Dragons: Predators of the Prehistoric Oceans* by Richard Ellis (Lawrence: University Press of Kansas, 2003), which nicely summarizes the major groups of sea dragons and recent scientific discoveries about them. Shortly after the publication of *Sea Dragons*, Mike Everhart wrote *Oceans of Kansas: A Natural History of the Western Interior Sea* (Bloomington: Indiana University Press, 2005). *Oceans of Kansas* doesn't just talk about sea dragons. It covers all aspects of life in the inland sea that once covered central North America. Together these books give a wonderful overview of ancient marine reptiles and their world. Both titles are written for adults, but if you're a reptile nut like I am, you won't have any trouble reading them.

If these two books don't quench your Mesozoic thirst, also check out *Dinosaurs, Spitfires, and Sea Dragons* by Christopher McGowan (Cambridge, MA: Harvard University Press, 1991). It's a bit more technical than the others, but still very readable. If you can find it in your library, you might also want to read a much older book, *Extinct Monsters: A Popular Account of Some of the Larger Forms of Ancient Animal Life* by Rev. H. N. Hutchinson (New York: D. Appleton and company, 1892). It's fascinating to see how scientists were thinking over one hundred years ago—and impressive how knowledgeable many early scientists were about ancient marine reptiles.

Websites

There are several terrific websites about ancient marine reptiles. All URLs were accurate at the time of publication.

Oceans of Kansas
http://www.oceansofkansas.com

You could spend days on this site, based on the book *Oceans of Kansas*, and never get bored. It was put together by that book's author, Mike Everhart, and contains information about virtually every aspect of ancient marine reptiles, with special attention given to those that lived in the inland seas of North America.

The Plesiosaur Site
http://www.plesiosaur.com/

This is a wonderful introductory site devoted to plesiosaurs. It is designed and maintained by paleontologist and researcher Richard Forrest, and debunks many myths about these animals.

The Ichthyosaur Page
http://www.ucmp.berkeley.edu/people/motani/ichthyo/index.html

This is part of the University of California at Berkeley site and is maintained by paleontologist Ryosuke Motani. All the latest knowledge about ichthyosaurs is summarized here, including the different types and what made them special.

Visit the Sea Dragons for Yourself!

If you think sea dragons are as fascinating as I do, you'll of course want to see some of them for yourself. You're in luck, because several museums in the United States and Canada house excellent collections of fossils and reconstructed ancient marine reptiles.

The Academy of Natural Sciences in Philadelphia has a wonderful collection of sea dragons, including Edward Drinker Cope's famous "backward plesiosaur."
> 1900 Benjamin Franklin Parkway
> Philadelphia, PA 19103 USA
> (215) 299-1000
> http://www.ansp.org/museum/index.php

The University of Nebraska State Museum has an entire gallery on the Mesozoic era, including plesiosaur and mosasaur fossils.
> 307 Morrill Hall, University of Nebraska–Lincoln
> Lincoln, NE 68588-0338 USA
> (402) 472-2642
> http://www-museum.unl.edu/

The Sternberg Museum of Natural History was named after the Sternberg family, some of North America's greatest fossil hunters. This museum's focus is on the wealth of life living in the Cretaceous period, and includes displays on mosasaurs, plesiosaurs, and many other fascinating marine and land animals.

> 3000 Sternberg Drive
> Hays, KS 67601 USA
> (877) 332-1165
> http://www.fhsu.edu/sternberg/index.shtml

The Peabody Museum of Natural History located at Yale University displays ichthyosaurs, plesiosaurs, and mosasaurs, as well as many dinosaur skeletons and fossils.

> Yale University
> 170–210 Whitney Avenue
> New Haven, CT 06511 USA
> (203) 432-5050
> http://www.peabody.yale.edu/

The Denver Museum of Nature and Science has two fine plesiosaurs displayed, along with a mosasaur, an ichthyosaur, and other ancient marine reptiles.

> 2001 Colorado Boulevard
> Denver, CO 80205 USA
> (303) 322-7009 or (800) 925-2250
> http://www.dmns.org/

The Berlin-Ichthyosaur State Park is located twenty-three miles east of Gabbs, Nevada. It is the site of some of North America's best—and biggest—ichthyosaur discoveries. During much of the year, the park provides regular tours of a fossil house that gives a sense of what these early fossil digs were like.

> HC 61 Box 61200
> Austin, NV 89310 USA
> (775) 964-2440
> http://parks.nv.gov/bi.htm

The Royal Tyrrell Museum, about a ninety-minute drive from Calgary, Alberta, has a wonderful collection of all the sea dragon groups, with plans to exhibit at least part of the world's largest ichthyosaur, *Shonisaurus sikanniensis*.

> Hwy 838 Midland Provincial Park
> Drumheller, Alberta
> Canada   T0J 0Y0
> (888) 440-4240
> http://www.tyrrellmuseum.com/

Glossary

Adaptation—a change that occurs in a species to allow it to survive better in its environment

Ammonite—a kind of cephalopod common during the Mesozoic era. Ammonites are known for their coiled shells that are divided into chambers filled with air.

Belemnite—a Mesozoic cephalopod characterized by a long straight shell and suckers with hooks in them

Cephalopods—animals including squid, octopuses, and nautiluses that have no backbones and have many arms with suckers for grasping. Ancient forms include ammonites and belemnites.

Cretaceous period—the last of the three periods of the Mesozoic era; it extended from approximately 146 million to 65 million years ago.

Countershading—a color scheme found in many marine animals in which their top surfaces are dark and their bottom surfaces are pale. This allows them to be camouflaged when viewed from above and below.

Echolocation—a method of hunting and navigation found in bats and marine mammals, by which an animal makes sounds and then listens to the returning echoes. This allows animals to detect prey and other surrounding objects.

Ectothermic—relying on the sun or other external heat sources to power digestion and other bodily processes; cold-blooded.

Elasmosaurs—the Mesozoic group of plesiosaurs that includes animals with very long necks

Endothermic—generating heat and energy through chemical processes instead of relying on the sun or other external energy sources; warm-blooded.

Evolution—the process by which species change over time via mutations that happen in their DNA. This is how new species are created from older ones.

Extinction—the permanent disappearance, or death, of every individual of an entire species

Food web—the complex relationship among species in a habitat. In a food web, some species are producers while others are predators or grazers.

Fossil—the remains or traces of a species that lived in the geological past. Usually only bones, teeth, and other hard parts are preserved as fossils.

Gastroliths—rocks or stones that are swallowed to aid in crushing food in the digestive tract

Ichthyosaurs—a group of Mesozoic marine reptiles that, in their most advanced forms, resembled today's dolphins; often called fish-lizards.

Jurassic period—the second of the three periods of the Mesozoic era; it extended from approximately 206 million to 146 million years ago.

K-T extinction event, or End Cretaceous Event—the disastrous event that led to the extinction of 85 percent of earth's species, including the last of the sea dragons. K-T stands for Cretaceous-Tertiary and defines the boundary between these two periods. (K is an abbreviation for the German word for Cretaceous.)

Mesozoic era—the time in Earth's history that extended from about 245 million to 65 million years ago

Monitor lizards—a group of about thirty modern lizard species, including the Komodo dragon, that feature long bodies and several other snakelike features

Mosasaurs—the last great group of ancient marine reptiles, known for being highly adaptable and having long, bendy bodies

Opalized—changed into an opal through a process by which silica replaces other substances in rock, bone, and other tissues to produce semiprecious gems

Palate—the roof of the mouth

Paleontology—the study of life-forms of past geological periods as known through fossil remains

Paleozoic Era—the period in Earth's history from 545 million to 245 million years ago

Permian period—the last period of the Paleozoic era, coming immediately before the Mesozoic era; it extended from about 290 million to about 245 million years ago.

Plesiosaurs—a group of ancient marine reptiles that includes the long-necked elasmosaurs and the shorter-necked pliosaurs. Scientists also recognize a third group called the polycotlids.

Pliosaurs—a group of plesiosaurs featuring short necks, large skulls, and bone-crushing jaws

Sclerotic ring—a circle of bony plates found in the eye sockets of some fishes and birds, and some living and extinct reptiles. Scientists believe that the ring changes the focus of the eye by pushing against the eyeball, changing its shape.

Serrated—notched or toothed like a saw blade

Triassic period—the first of the three periods of the Mesozoic era; it extended from approximately 245 million to 208 million years ago.

Tylosaurs—a group of especially large, dominant mosasaurs

Vertebrae—the individual bones that comprise a spine, or backbone

Index

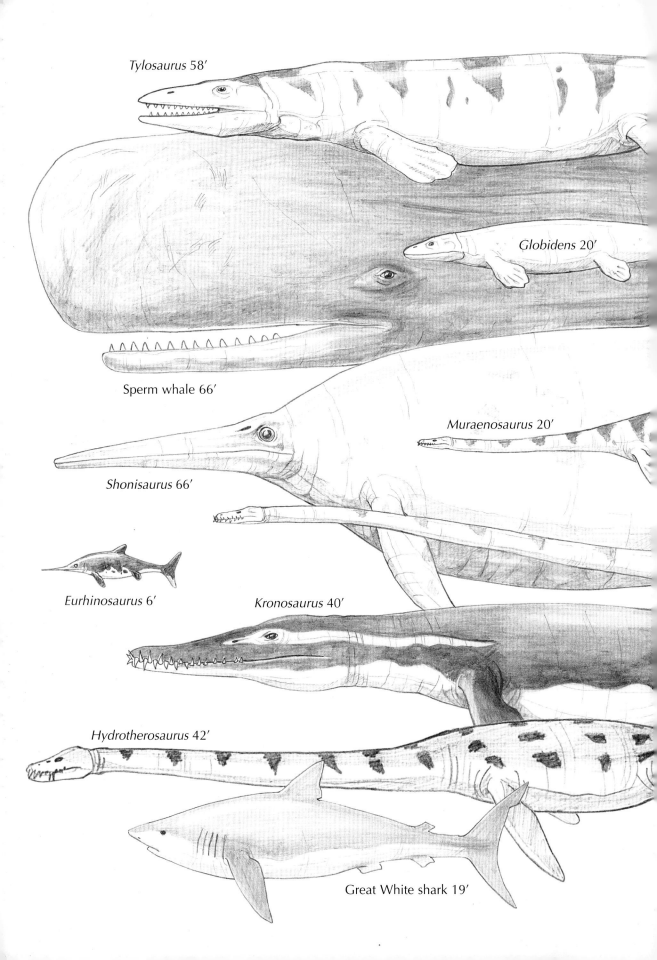

Tylosaurus 58'

Globidens 20'

Sperm whale 66'

Muraenosaurus 20'

Shonisaurus 66'

Eurhinosaurus 6'

Kronosaurus 40'

Hydrotherosaurus 42'

Great White shark 19'

Clidastes 12'

Killer whale 33'

Umoonasaurus 7'

Elasmosaurus 47'

Peloneustes 10'

Temnodontosaurus 30'

Cryptoclidus 13'